Jonas Brothers
Yearbook 2010

POSY EDWARDS

Introducing:
THE JONAS BROTHERS

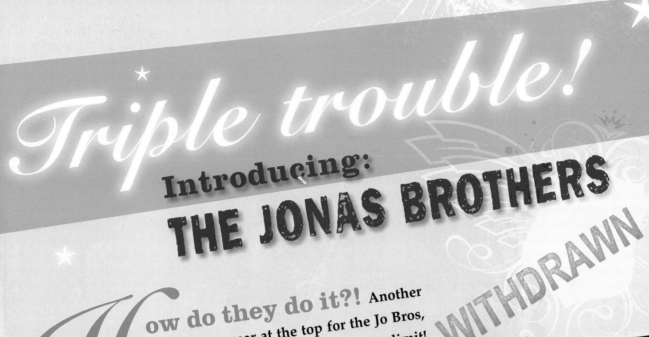

WITHDRAWN

How do they do it?! Another sparkling year at the top for the Jo Bros, and they're proving the sky's the limit! Kevin, Joe and Nick have sung, played and acted on stage and screen, stealing hearts across the world and it's not hard to see why. These boys have it all.

Kevin Jonas Senior and Denise Jonas must consider themselves to be the luckiest parents in the world – having sons who all possess incredible musical and acting talent, as well as being pretty fine to look at too!

Perhaps it's no wonder the boys have grown up so musical. Dad Kevin taught songwriting at bible college, and mum Denise was a singer who worked in the school's office. They would take singing groups on the road, and took the boys with them when they travelled. When they

5

were at home, the boys would hang around the piano for hours, making up songs and singing together.

All three brothers were really musical from a young age, especially Nick, who was "discovered" at just six years old, singing in a local barber's where he was getting a haircut. When he was just seven, Nick began performing in musicals on Broadway – amazing for a kid so young!

Nick wrote and released a song with his dad in 2003, and then released a solo album that he, Joe and Kevin had all written songs for. At the same time, Joe was following in his little bro's footsteps, and performing on Broadway too, and Kevin was auditioning for bands. Columbia Records liked what they heard and decided to sign the boys as a group act, and now they're one of the hottest bands around. Thank you Columbia!

THE BIG TIME

Nick, Joe and Kevin thought about calling themselves "Sons of Jonas", but finally decided on the name "Jonas Brothers". They toured in 2005 and started work on their album *It's About Time*, which was supposed to be released in February 2006 but was pushed back several times, finally coming out in August 2006.

Nick's solo single was re-released, and the boys toured again with Aly & AJ. Their single "Year 3000" became a hit on Radio Disney, but the Jonas Brothers were dropped by their label in early 2007, which totally upset their fanbase.

But, thankfully, they didn't stay without a label for long: the Jonas Brothers signed with Hollywood Records in February 2007 and the boys were in more demand than ever. Around the same time, the boys began appearing in adverts on TV, singing jingles. They worked on a new album, called *Jonas Brothers*, which was released later that year, and also made a whole host of television and live appearances.

In 2008 they performed on their first headline US tour, as well as opening for Avril Lavigne's European tour. They also released a third album, *A Little Bit Longer*, set off on another headline tour called *The Burning Up Tour*, starred in the Disney Channel hit movie, *Camp Rock*, and started filming their own TV series, *JONAS*. Phew! Busy times for those Jonas Brothers!

SCHOOL TIME

When they were younger, our boys had to go to school, just like everyone else. And just like everyone else, they suffered the same problems – homework, and even bullying.

"I thought the popular kids were the cool kids. I got caught up in that, and it was bogus. High school is about finding who you are because that's more important than trying to be someone else." – Nick

As their touring schedule is so hectic, all three brothers have been home-schooled at some time or other. Kevin and Joe originally attended Kevin Eastern Christian High School in North Haledon, New Jersey. Kevin was home-schooled after his second year in high school, while Joe was in the seventh grade.

jonas brothers

But they still have their likes and dislikes when it comes to schoolwork!

Kevin's favourite subjects are History and Latin, Physical Science and Chemistry. Joe loves Mathematics, Physics and Social Science, and Nick's really into Spelling and Geology. But the boys have their hates too – Kevin hates school because you have to get up so early. Joe hates bullies, and Nick hates Mathematics!

The boys are maturing though, and it's not totally out of the question that they might want to go to college one day, although how they'll do any work with crowds of screaming girls chasing them everywhere, who knows! Kevin and Joe have their eyes on Berkeley School of Music, while Nick's interested in going to Northwestern University: these guys have brains too!

HOME LIFE

Although they may be huge music and movie stars now, the Jonas Brothers have always been respectful and down-to-earth. They play pranks on each other just like all siblings do, and at home (or around the tour bus!) they do chores like taking out the trash and helping their parents out. What good guys!

The Jonas Quiz!

How much do you really know about these brothers? Take the test and see if you're their number one fan!

1. Which brother has which birthday?
a) 5 November 1987
b) 16 September 1992
c) 15 August 1989
d) 28 September 2000

2. What is Nick's most ticklish spot?
a) His ears
b) His armpits
c) His feet
d) His neck

3. Where was Joe born?
a) Casa Grande, Arizona
b) Hollywood, California
c) London, UK
d) Sydney, Australia

4. Kevin loves being the oldest, because it means he:
a) Is the tallest
b) Can eat before his brothers do
c) Can decide what songs they will play
d) Can boss his brothers around

5. Which of these is the title of a Jonas Brothers album?
a) It's About Rhyme
b) It's About Time
c) It's About Pizza
d) It's About My Dog

6. Where did Joe go for his first holiday?
a) France
b) England
c) Canada
d) Mexico

7. Who is Kevin's favourite actor?
a) James Dean
b) Orlando Bloom
c) Johnny Depp
d) Will Smith

8. From what film was the first song that Nick ever sang?
a) Beauty and the Beast
b) The Little Mermaid
c) Peter Pan
d) The Jungle Book

9. To get pumped up before a show, what do the boys do on the tour bus?
a) Have a dance party – turning everything up as loud as it will go
b) Eat a huge pizza each
c) Clean the toilet
d) Make their beds

10. Which of the following does Kevin have an obsession with?
a) McDonalds
b) Burger King
c) Starbucks
d) KFC

11. What is Nick's favourite colour?
a) Green
b) Yellow
c) Black
d) Blue

12. Which of these movies does Joe totally love?
a) *High School Musical*
b) *Chitty Chitty Bang Bang*
c) *Shrek*
d) *Bambi*

13. Which of the following does Nick suffer from?
a) Myopia
b) Anosmia
c) Diabetes
d) Deafness

14. What is the most embarrassing thing that's happened to Kevin onstage?
a) His shoe coming off
b) Falling off the stage
c) Messing up his guitar solo
d) Not realising the song had ended

15. The Jonas Brothers have a little brother who is not in the band – what is his name?
a) Frankie
b) Johnny
c) Randy
d) Paddy

16. Where does Nick spend too much money?
a) The iTunes store
b) Denny's
c) At the mall
d) On shoes

17. In *Camp Rock*, what is the name of the band the Jonas Brothers are in?
a) Chess
b) Battleships
c) Connect Three
d) Connect Four

18. What is Nick's least favourite school subject?
a) Geography
b) History
c) English
d) Mathematics

19. What is the name of Joe Jonas's character in *Camp Rock*?
a) Shane Gray
b) Mark White
c) Fred Brown
d) John Orange

20. What are the Jonas parents called?
a) Frankie Nick Jonas Senior and Dina Jonas
b) Paul Kevin Jonas Senior and Daisy Jonas
c) Paul Kevin Jonas Senior and Denise Jonas
d) Kevin Joe Jonas Senior and Debbie Jonas

Now check out your answers on Page 62

13

Kevin can't go to sleep without making his bed first. Even if it's been made in the morning, he has to remake it! It's his quirky habit. Kevin never has any trouble sleeping but he loves to stay up late.

KEVIN

Being the oldest, Kevin has always done everything his parents ask him to do, and tries to help as much as possible. With another three sons, it's no wonder his parents probably needed a little help sometimes! Kevin is very protective of his family, and he's often a source of advice when Joe, Nick or youngest brother Frankie are facing a new and tough situation – Kevin's almost certainly faced it before!

14

JOE

According to his mum, Joe was quiet as a child, but he's certainly outgrown that now, as the loudest, messiest and laziest Jonas Brother! When he was younger he never thought about singing, instead he thought he would like to be a comedian, but like his brothers, he sang in the church choir. And after performing in three Broadway productions, it became clear he had talents in other areas too. Today Joe is most known for his random sayings and crazy dances . . . oh yeah, and also for playing the lead in the hot Disney movie, *Camp Rock!*

15

NICK

As a child, Nick was very creative and independent. He gets upset when things go wrong or when he doesn't do well. He says he used to be very uptight, but he's learned to loosen up. And with such great brothers, it's no wonder! Nick says the main thing that makes him laugh is his brothers goofing around, but he hates it when his brothers take his stuff. Nick shares a bedroom with his younger brother Frankie, and he keeps his closet surprisingly clean! In November 2005, Nick Jonas found out that he had Type 1 diabetes. He's managing fine these days and is busy providing inspiration for kids suffering with diabetes everywhere. "Don't let it slow you down at all," is his message. "Just keep a positive attitude and keep moving forward with it!"

The fourth brother!

He might not be part of the Jonas Brothers band, but young Bonus Jonas is also pretty musical – he's in his own band!

'Frank the Tank' or 'Bonus Jonas' was born in the boys' hometown of Wyckoff, New Jersey. He has dark hair and brown eyes just like his older brothers. Joe was so excited when his younger brother Frankie was born that on the first night home from the hospital, Joe woke up to help his mother with feeding and diaper changing. What a great brother!

Little Frankie knows how to play the guitar, and wants to learn to play drums too. His older brothers asked him if he wanted to be in their band, but he said he was going to start one of his own! Frankie's band is called Hollywood Shake Up – he used to be in a band called Drop/Slap. He has no plans to join his brothers' band when he gets older – he's happy rocking on his own! His favourite song is 'That's Just the Way We Roll' from the album *Jonas Brothers*. He also appears alongside his brothers in the show *JONAS*.

Although he's yet to achieve the superstardom of his brothers, Frankie already has celebrity friends – he video-chats with Miley Cyrus's little sister, Noah. And speaking of Miley Cyrus, the *Hannah Montana* star is Frankie's secret celebrity crush! His older brother Nick once said that he thought Miley was cute and Frankie tried to beat him up. What a sweetie!

BONUS JONAS FACTS

Full name: Franklin Nathaniel Jonas

Birthday: 28 September 2000

Current home: LA, California

Favourite holiday: Christmas

Favourite show: *The Suite Life of Zack and Cody*

Frankie is a huge baseball fan and supports the New York Yankees

Copy a picture

Take a picture with Nick

What would you like to ask Nick?

Friends

See more friends

Nick Jonas

Facts   **Info**   **Extras**

Full name: Nicholas Jerry Jonas

Date of birth: 16 September 1992

Place of birth: Dallas, Texas

Star sign: Virgo

Chinese horoscope sign: Monkey

Hobbies: Music, song-writing, baseball, collecting baseball cards, tennis, golf

Instruments: Guitar, drums, piano

Favourite food: Steak

Favourite ice cream: Cotton Candy

Favourite sport: Baseball

Nick would like to live in Chicago someday

Jonas Brothers COLOURING PAGE

Nick

Copy a picture
Take a picture with Joe

What would you like to ask Joe?

Friends

See more friends

Joe Jonas

Facts   Info   Extras

Full name: Joseph Adam Jonas

Date of birth: 15 August 1989

Place of birth: Casa Grande, Arizona

Star sign: Leo

Chinese horoscope sign: Snake

Hobbies: Making movies, jogging and working out

Instruments: Guitar, piano, percussion (tambourine!)

Favourite food: Chicken cutlet sandwich with mayonnaise

Favourite colour: Blue

Favourite ice cream: Chocolate Marshmallow

Favourite sport: Wiffleball

Jonas Brothers COLOURING PAGE

Joe

🖱 Copy a picture
🖱 Take a picture with Kevin

Kevin Jonas

Facts   **Info**   **Extras**

Full name: Paul Kevin Jonas II

Date of birth: 5 November 1987

Place of birth: Teaneck, New Jersey

Star sign: Scorpio

Chinese horoscope sign: Rabbit

Hobbies: Playing guitar and bowling

Instruments: Guitar

Favourite food: Sushi

Favourite colour: Green

Favourite ice cream: Rocky Road

Favourite sport: Pole Vaulting

What would you like to ask Kevin?

Friends

See more friends

Jonas Brothers COLOURING PAGE

Kevin

Love & Romance

Recently, the Jo Bros have been romantically linked with some seriously hot Hollywood talent – Taylor Swift, Miley Cyrus, Selena Gomez, JoJo, Chelsea Staub and Amanda Michalka to name but a few – but today, we're happy to report all three brothers are single!

NICK

Nick has two modes when he's around girls – first he gets really quiet, but then he's the complete opposite, where he's telling jokes and clowning around. How he acts depends on the girl. "It helps when a girl's really confident because then I don't feel like I have to entertain her," he says. "What I'm looking for in a girl is someone who will understand my crazy schedule and will be there to support me. Just a girl who will make me smile and keep me happy."

JOE

As for Joe, the first thing he notices about his crush is her eyes. He likes a girl to have natural beauty – he isn't into girls that wear a lot of make-up. Fashion-wise, he likes it when girls wear leggings. "I like girls who have a cool sense of fashion and don't mind standing out a bit," he says. Joe also thinks that looks aren't as important as attitude. He likes girls who like to have fun, especially if they're talented. In his opinion, every girl has something special about her! According to Joe, "The best thing a girl can do to show she cares about a guy is to support what he likes to do." So keep turning up to those shows! He also likes girls to write him letters. But at the end of the day, a girl has to pass the biggest test of all: Joe's parents must like her too. "If Mom likes a girl, then it's all good," he says! Aw!

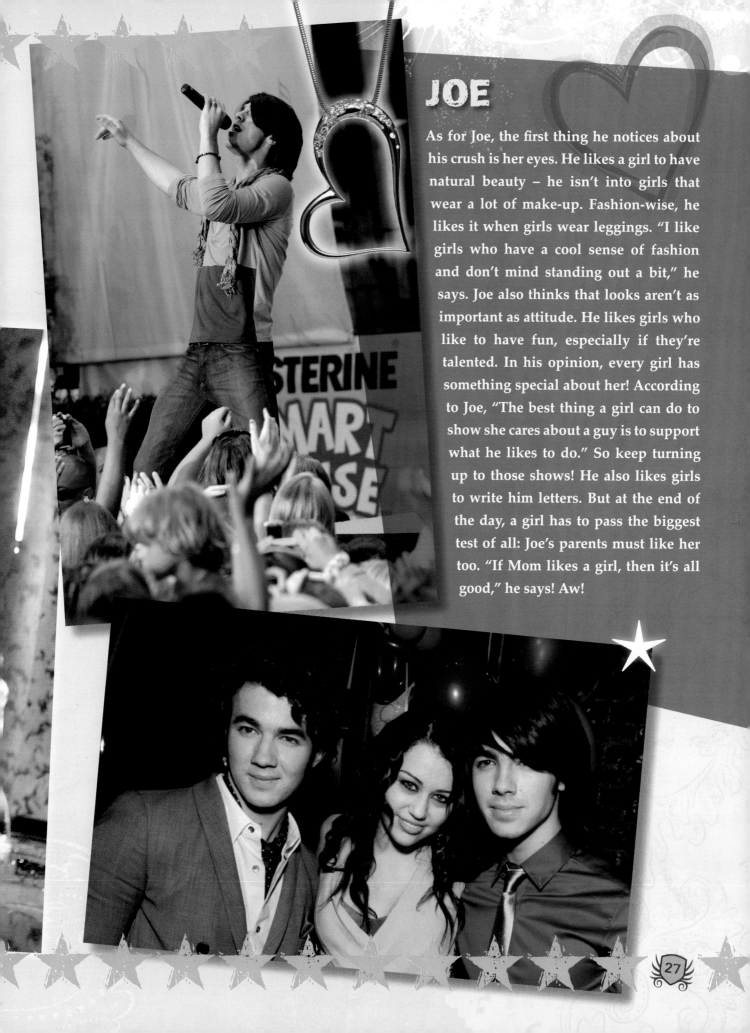

KEVIN

Being the oldest, Kevin has tons more embarrassing date stories than his brothers. "One time I took this girl out to eat at a really nice place in LA," he says. "We ordered a ton of food, but when the bill came, I realised I forgot my wallet at home! My dad had to come bring it to me. It was so embarrassing! I didn't think it was big deal, but Nick and Joe still tease me about it!" Once Kevin also had a girlfriend who would send back the notes he had written her with all his spelling errors circled – which really bummed him out! Ultimately, Kevin just wants a girlfriend who has a positive attitude and is easy-going – like him – and one that understands his crazy schedule!

Make a *Jonas Brothers* milkshake!

No, we're not suggesting you put your favourite brother in a blender – last year, Jo Bros visited a restaurant in New York called Olana and they loved the milkshakes there so much they wanted to meet the chef!
Want to make your own amazing Olana Jo Bros milkshake? Then get mixing with the recipe below! Yum!

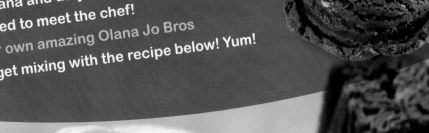

Olana Jonas Brothers Chocolate Milkshake
Serves 3, of course!

6 scoops chocolate ice cream
3 tbsp dark chocolate fondue (*recipe below)
1 ½ cups milk
¼ cup brownies
½ cup whipped cream
2 tbsp chocolate chips

To make the chocolate fondue:
2 fluid oz of heavy cream
3 oz (90g) chopped dark chocolate
1 tsp sugar
A pinch of salt

Melt the chocolate and combine with the cream, sugar and salt

Preparation: Combine the chocolate ice cream, fondue, milk, and brownies in a blender. Blend until smooth. Pour into chilled glasses and top with whipped cream and chocolate chips.

Then just sit back and slurp!

Which *Jonas Brother* are

You may have your favourite, but take this quiz to see which Jonas brother you're destined to date! **You may be surprised by the answers...**

1. My ideal date would be
a) Sitting by the lake while he sings me a song he wrote for me
b) Running around causing trouble at a fairground
c) Hanging out and having a coffee

2. If I had to pick, I'd like a guy who was
a) Cute and sensitive
b) Cute and funny
c) Cute and romantic

3. Now for looks – what about that head of hair?
a) It's all about those lovely curls
b) Straight – even if it means he has to borrow my straighteners!
c) Straight or curly, however the mood takes me

4. And how about the wardrobe? I like
a) A guy who always wears a vest
b) Skinny jeans, braces and neon sunglasses
c) A sharp suit and tie, even just watching TV

5. Break-ups are really sad, but here's how I handle mine:

a) Easy – I just go out with their sworn enemy

b) "Hi, how are you, let's break up. Bye!"

c) I don't believe in break-ups!

6. If my man could do any job in the world he would be

a) The president of a huge record company

b) Job? He'd never have a job – he's too charming for that!

c) A rich businessman raking in lots of cash

7. If I was going to date someone from a band, they would be

a) A hot drummer/singer/songwriter

b) A gorgeous dancing lead-singer

c) A totally cool guitarist

8. Personality-wise, my ideal guy is

a) A smart, sensitive guy who makes me swoon

b) A fun-lovin' goofball who loves to party

c) The strong, sensible protective one

Did you answer mostly:

A? Then you're destined to date Nick Jonas! The baby of the band, Nick is intelligent and often comes across as more mature than his two brothers.

B? Fasten your seatbelt – your perfect match is Joe Jonas! This fun-loving goofball will definitely keep you entertained.

C? You've got mature taste, which is probably why you picked oldest brother Kevin. The strong, protective member of the group, Kevin takes care of his own, and loves a good latte.

Camp Rock ROCKS!

You'd have to have been on a different planet not to have seen *Camp Rock* at least ten times by now! Disney's awesome modern-day Cinderella tale set in a summer music-camp confirmed that the Jonas Brothers had arrived – and as well as stealing the show on the airwaves, they are now kings of the silver screen!

Camp Rock Fact: Certain scenes were filmed on location at Camp Wanakita, and Camp Kilcoo in the Haliburton Highlands, Ontario, Canada

"My character is out there, a little spacey, but I love it. I get to be a little loopy, and it's kinda fun. Nick plays the leader in the group, which is really true. He always keeps me in line – me and Joe are always goofing around. I'm always just having a good time; Joe is goofing off."

Kevin Jonas

34

CAMP ROCK: *The story*

Camp Rock is the story of Mitchie Torres (played by Demi Lovato), who has an amazing singing voice and desperately wants to go to a prestigious summer rock-camp. Her family can't afford to send her, but realising how much her daughter wants to go, Mitchie's mother gets a job as a cook there and takes Mitchie with her, as long as she helps out in the kitchen between classes.

Mitchie is befriended by fellow camp member Caitlyn (Alyson Stoner), and spends her time living a double life at the camp: posing as a well-off camper, and hiding the fact she is the cook's daughter. Her secret is discovered, but when she is overheard singing (but not seen) by teen pop star and celebrity camp instructor Shane Gray (Joe Jonas), he is completely taken and sets out to find the girl behind the beautiful voice. Meanwhile, Mitchie will have to learn how to confront her fears, step out of the kitchen and into the spotlight as herself.

Camp Rock Fact: While the brothers were in Canada filming *Camp Rock*, Nick had a day when his blood sugar was a little out of control. He says he was "kind of bumming. I walked by this room in the hotel we were staying at, and it was so weird, all of a sudden there was this big ballroom with a piano in it. It was like a scene out of a movie. So I went in there, sat down at the piano and wrote a song. Later on I played it for the cast, and they all loved it."

THE JONAS CONNECTION

Although Joe takes the leading role, there's enough of Kevin and Nick to keep Jonas Brothers' fans happy! "I wanted to see more of my brothers in the movie, too, because they were so good in it," says Joe. Nick points out that doing their first movie was "an extreme opportunity" they were so excited to have.

All three brothers agree that the one thing that drew them to the movie was the music. "We listened to the songs. We thought the music was something that was really interesting to us. Especially the song we did with the band Connect Three. That's maybe a song that we would do one day. So it all kind of worked out. It was good!" says Nick. The movie's spectacular soundtrack is sure to have you bouncing around your room and practising dance moves all year long!

CHARACTERS

Shane Gray (Joe Jonas) has the lead male role in the movie. He is the singer of the band Connect Three, who originally met and formed at Camp Rock. Now a successful rock star, Shane messes up by storming off the set of a music-video shoot. Connect Three cancel their summer tour and send him to rock 'n' roll camp to get his bearings and find himself again.

The other two band members are Nate and Jason (Nick and Kevin Jonas), who – in the movie – aren't related at all, unlike in real life! Nate (Nick Jonas) is Shane and Jason's best friend and band member. He is the guitarist and vocalist of the band Connect Three. Nick's character is sort of bossy – like Nick in real life, says Joe!

Jason (Kevin Jonas) is Shane and Nate's best friend and band member. He is the lead guitarist of the band Connect Three, and his character is not too bright – Kevin is hilarious at playing an airhead!

"The biggest challenge of doing the movie was acting in general. It's so new to us. We're so used to performing onstage. I didn't know how I would do. Honestly, I got kind of nervous! But I felt really comfortable about halfway through."

Joe Jonas

CAST

Joe Jonas as Shane Gray
Nick Jonas as Nate
Kevin Jonas as Jason
Demi Lovato as Mitchie Torres
Meaghan Jette Martin as Tess Tyler
Alyson Stoner as Caitlyn Geller
Anna Maria Perez de Taglé as Ella

CROSSWORD

ACROSS

2. What Nick, Joe and Kevin thought of calling their band first
3. Kevin's place of birth
4. The Jonas Brothers' hometown
6. The school subject Nick hates
9. Joe's favourite colour
10. The name of the fourth Jonas brother
11. Nick's middle name

DOWN

1. The name of the band the Jonas Brothers are part of in *Camp Rock*
2. Nick's favourite food
5. The name of the Jonas Brothers' biggest fan on *J.O.N.A.S*
7. Joe Jonas's character in *Camp Rock*
8. Kevin's Chinese horoscope sign

Answers on pg 62

OTHER TALENT

The movie features a whole gang of talented tween stars that are sure to hit the same stardom as the cast of *High School Musical*: among them, Demi Lovato, Alyson Stoner, Meaghan Jette Martin, Anna Maria Perez de Taglé, Jasmine Richards and Maria Canals-Barrera. Watch this space...

Camp Rock's Message:

ON THE SET

According to the boys, the Canadian set where the movie was filmed was so beautiful, they loved it. "We'd sneak into one of the boats and take off or sit on the dock and hang out. It felt like we were really at camp!" says Joe. The brothers definitely made friends with their fellow cast members. As soon as the filming for the movie was over, the cast really missed each other – just as if they had actually gone home from summer camp!

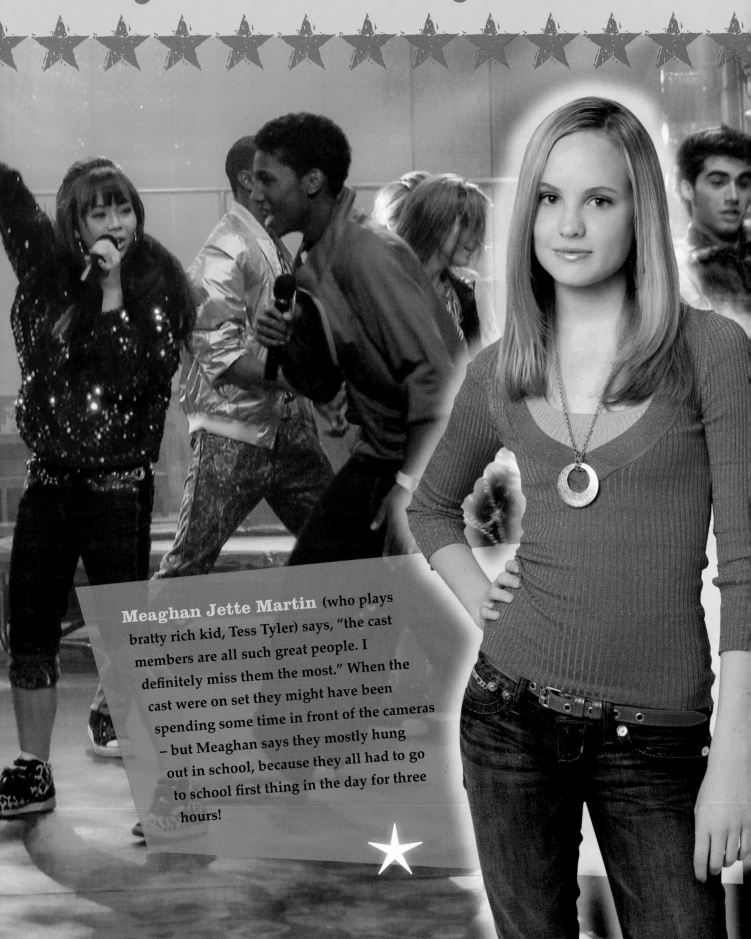

"Stay true to who you are"

Meaghan Jette Martin (who plays bratty rich kid, Tess Tyler) says, "the cast members are all such great people. I definitely miss them the most." When the cast were on set they might have been spending some time in front of the cameras – but Meaghan says they mostly hung out in school, because they all had to go to school first thing in the day for three hours!

"I ♥ Joe!"

You will need:
Lots of old magazines with pictures of your favourite Jonas brother or all three of them
Old badges
Scissors
Glue
Coloured pens

"Nick's the best"

MAKE YOUR OWN
Jonas Brothers BADGE!

Show your devotion to your favourite Jonas brother with an awesome home-made badge!

"Kevin rules!"

Instructions:

1. Choose a badge that's a similar size to the face in one of your pictures.

2. Place the badge over the picture of the face and use your scissors to cut out the picture of your favourite brother around the badge.

3. Using your glue, stick the picture on the badge.

4. With a colourful pen write things like

   JoBros Rock!

   or your name and their's on the badge.

5. If you want, you could stick your picture on the badge next to their face.

44

"Jonas Bros 4ever!"

DESIGN A T-SHIRT
FOR YOUR FAVOURITE BROTHER!

Everyone knows that the Jonas Brothers are the best-dressed boys in the music business. Here you can use your fashion sense plus your knowledge of the boys to design each one their very own t-shirt!

Tips: why not use each brother's favourite colour as a background to start you off – Nick and Joe's favourite colour is blue, and Kevin's favourite colour is green.

Happy designing and colouring!

45

Busy Boys

★

The Jo Bros sure like to keep busy. They totally smashed the charts in 2008 with their massive platinum-selling album, *A Little Bit Longer*, and two tours that earned the band a spot among the top-selling tours of the year. They also won an American Music Award for Breakthrough Artist, were nominated for a Grammy in the Best New Artist Category and won a Nickelodeon Kids' Choice award for best music group. Wow! So far in 2009 they have recorded a new album, filmed a TV series and rewarded their fans with a massive world tour! They've also dedicated some time to some of their less-fortunate fans, stopping for example in Texas to visit Jayla Cooper, a nine-year-old girl battling leukemia. Those brothers have hearts of gold, and are so down-to-earth – more reasons for us to totally love them!

But how do they find time to squeeze in all this ... and still have as much fun as they do? I guess that must be a **Jonas family secret!**

47

Jonas Brothers World Tour 2009

The **huge** world tour sees the brothers travelling to places like Mexico, Peru, Chile, Argentina, all across America, to Madrid, Paris, London, Barcelona, Berlin, Manchester, Dublin, and beyond!

The Jo Bros are really excited about travelling and coming face to face with millions of new fans – they totally love visiting new places and seeing new faces! "We want to see all of our fans in the US and also see all our new fans from around the world," says Joe. "We wish we could go everywhere. We are doing our best to hit as many places as possible."

Special guests on *The Jonas Brothers World Tour 2009* included *American Idol* winner and Jive Records' platinum-selling artist, Jordin Sparks, and rising stars, Honor Society. Demi Lovato also made a special appearance for a couple of shows which were promo shows for the boys' album, *Lines, Vines and Trying Times*. What a line-up!

According to Kevin, they planned the tour to feature songs from the album *Lines, Vines and Trying Times*, as well as including songs from their TV show, *JONAS*. That's a lot to squeeze into a show, but the Jo Bros always do their best for their fans. One thing they won't be doing is taking their shirts off though – the Jo Bros are down-to-earth and respectful, and know their limits. "We don't think that's necessary to get the audience excited," says Nick.

"I don't know about taking our shirts off right now – but maybe we'll wear short sleeves or tank tops!"

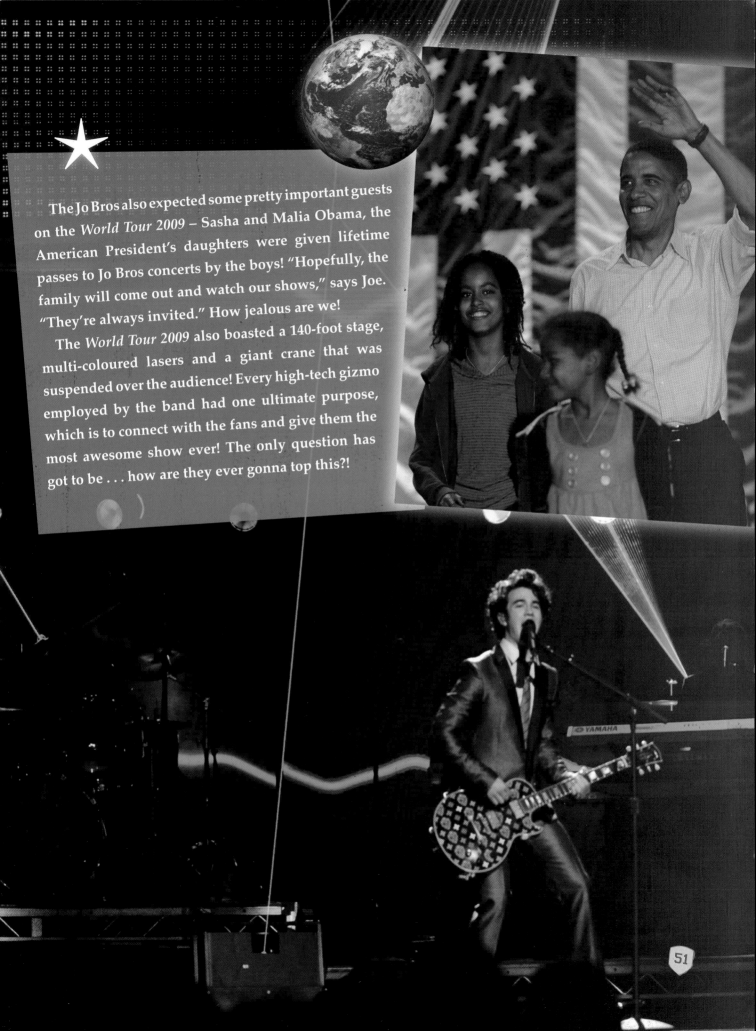

The Jo Bros also expected some pretty important guests on the *World Tour 2009* – Sasha and Malia Obama, the American President's daughters were given lifetime passes to Jo Bros concerts by the boys! "Hopefully, the family will come out and watch our shows," says Joe. "They're always invited." How jealous are we!

The *World Tour 2009* also boasted a 140-foot stage, multi-coloured lasers and a giant crane that was suspended over the audience! Every high-tech gizmo employed by the band had one ultimate purpose, which is to connect with the fans and give them the most awesome show ever! The only question has got to be . . . how are they ever gonna top this?!

Lines, Vines and Trying Times

Lines, Vines and Trying Times is the boys' fourth studio album – incredible when you think how young they all are! They started writing songs for the album in the summer of 2008, on their *Burning Up* tour.

The brothers have always been big fans of Europe, especially Britain! "We're being inspired by new music out of the UK," says Nick. The brothers also say that the Kings of Leon, Elvis Costello, The Zutons and Neil Diamond inspired their 2009 record.

Nick says the boys have "a lot of different inspirations, a lot of new sounds. We're just trying to continue to grow as musicians and songwriters." Nick goes on to say that the songs on the album are a peek into the journal of the Jonas boys, revealing to the fans all the things they've gone through, and personal experiences that they

get their inspiration from. Kevin adds: "The overall message is it's the same old Jonas Brothers, in a sense, but we're adding more and more music, including different musical instruments that are going to add and build to the sound we already have."

But where did they get that title from? "The title is a bit of poetry we came up with on the set for the TV show," dishes Nick. "Lines are something that someone feeds you, whether it's good or bad. Vines are the things that get in the way of the path that you're on, and trying times — well, obviously we're younger guys, but we're aware of what's going on in the world and we're trying to bring some light to it."

Judging by the song "Poison Ivy" – a tune about a toxic girl you can't resist – *Lines, Vines and Trying Times* is likely to follow previous Jonas successes and sell millions of copies worldwide!

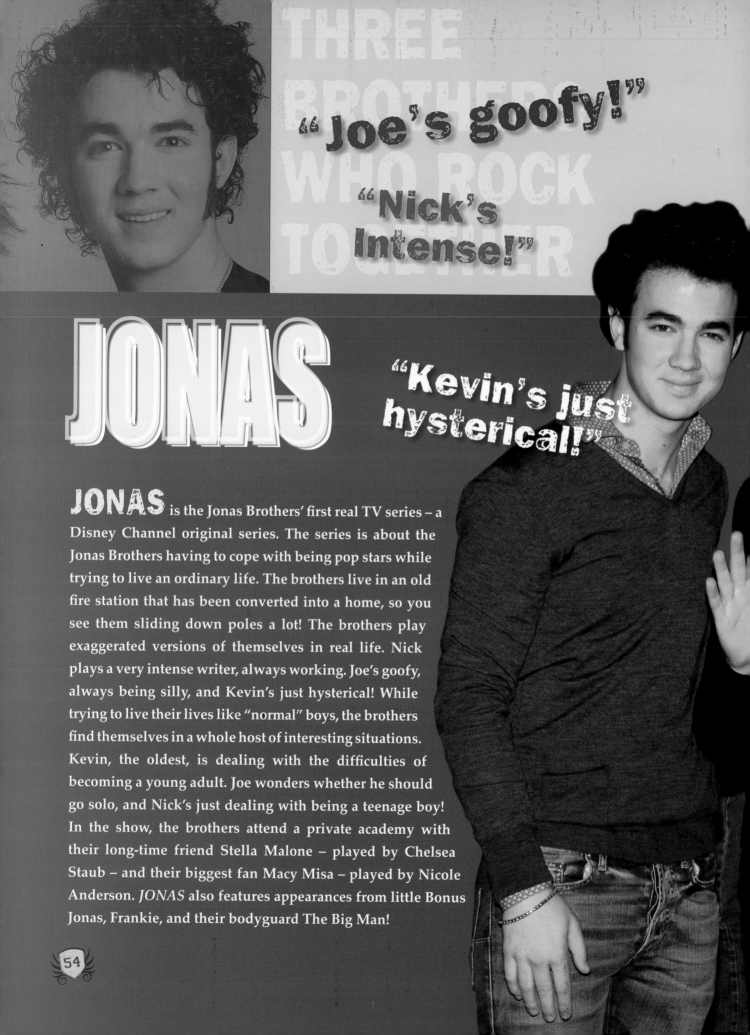

THREE BROTHERS WHO ROCK TOGETHER

"Joe's goofy!"

"Nick's Intense!"

JONAS

"Kevin's just hysterical!"

JONAS is the Jonas Brothers' first real TV series – a Disney Channel original series. The series is about the Jonas Brothers having to cope with being pop stars while trying to live an ordinary life. The brothers live in an old fire station that has been converted into a home, so you see them sliding down poles a lot! The brothers play exaggerated versions of themselves in real life. Nick plays a very intense writer, always working. Joe's goofy, always being silly, and Kevin's just hysterical! While trying to live their lives like "normal" boys, the brothers find themselves in a whole host of interesting situations. Kevin, the oldest, is dealing with the difficulties of becoming a young adult. Joe wonders whether he should go solo, and Nick's just dealing with being a teenage boy! In the show, the brothers attend a private academy with their long-time friend Stella Malone – played by Chelsea Staub – and their biggest fan Macy Misa – played by Nicole Anderson. *JONAS* also features appearances from little Bonus Jonas, Frankie, and their bodyguard The Big Man!

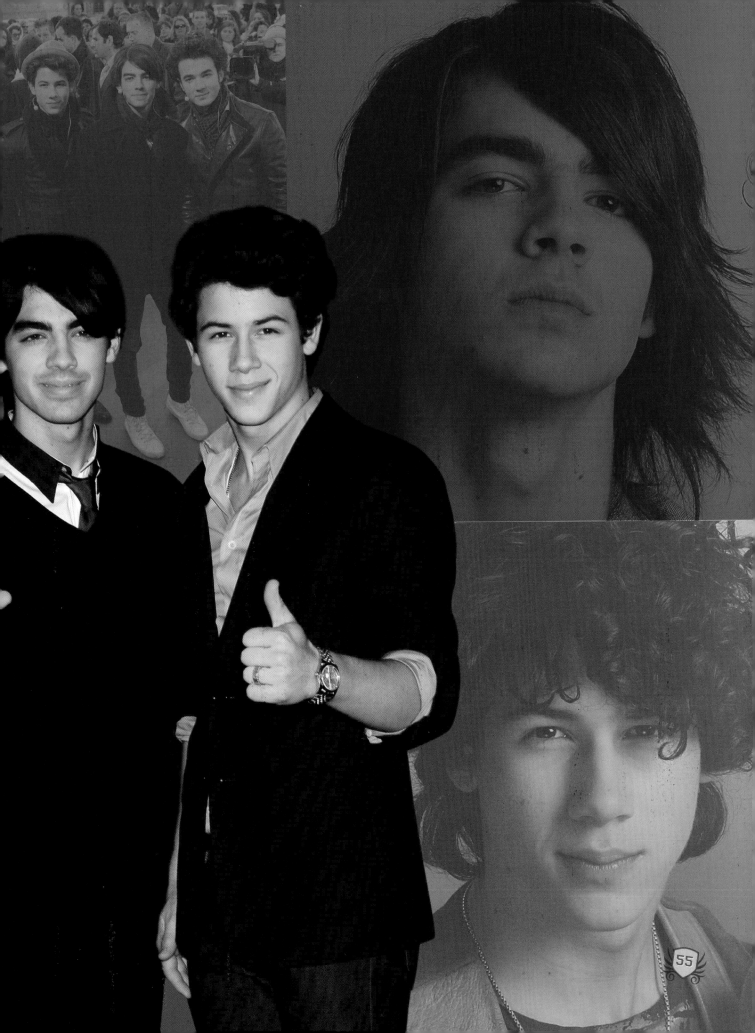

Jonas Brothers
Style Update

"I like to be a little more dressed up – I guess you could call it preppy, but I call it formal rock, because I have bright green shoes on, and I rolled up my sleeves, which is key." **Nick**

"You totally would see us in things like blazers, skinny ties and sparkly shoes even when we're not onstage. We like to dress up, and that was part of our goal. We always said we wanted to bring some high fashion back to rock 'n' roll!" **Kevin**

In case you hadn't noticed, the Jonas Brothers are the most stylish band on the planet. Always rocking the latest trends, it doesn't matter whether these boys are hanging out for a coffee, at the mall, or about to play in front of a million fans, they're always dressed to impress!

FASHION FACTS

Nick always wears a vest — and he loves his tie collection.

Joe's trademark is his headband, and he has hundreds of pairs of socks!

Kevin can't wait to come out with his own fashion line.

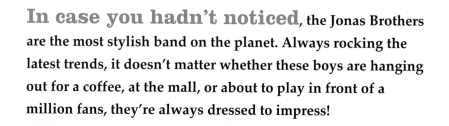

"If my brothers weren't there, I probably wouldn't get out of bed in the morning! I'm also always checking the mirror because I'm afraid that I have something in my teeth." **Joe**

Dress your *perfect* rock band!

So you think you could dress a rock band as well as the Jonas Brothers? Well here's your chance – the boys have got a huge concert tonight playing to thousands of fans, and they need the best threads they can find. It's down to you to make sure they look their best!

YOU WILL NEED:
Glue
Coloured pens
Scissors
Sheets of coloured paper

Instructions

1. First, you need inspiration. Have a look through all your magazines and on some websites to see what looks the Jo Bros are rocking. They're trend setters, and will be trying out something new almost every day! Remember each brother has his own individual style – Nick likes the "formal rock" look, Kevin likes to mix preppy with daytime wear, and as for Joe – he likes to mix it all up together and then wear sunglasses with it!

2. Once you've decided what each brother should wear, draw out your designs on the coloured paper. Cut the clothes out and use your coloured pens to add details. Glue them down to the Jonas Brothers' mannequins.

3. Now you need to decide on headwear. Are the brothers going to be wearing hats, or sunglasses? Design and cut out hats if you want them – and use your black pen to add sunglasses if the boys are going to be in serious rock mode!

4. And they're done! Which look is your favourite?

Joe likes to incorporate everything, but he loves the 80s for fashion.

Each member of the Jonas Brothers has his own individual style too: Nick likes to call his style formal rock, and says rolling up the sleeves is key.

Kevin aims for an almost Victorian dandy style, with collars. He likes wearing suits and he has to have shiny shoes all the time, even with sweatpants, which his brothers tease him about.

The future's bright

It seems impossible to imagine that 2010 could be even busier than this one for the Jonas Brothers, but they've already got a lot of projects in the pipeline. There's already talk of the follow-up album to *Lines, Vines and Trying Times*, yet ANOTHER world tour, and . . . wait for it . . . the sequel to the Disney smash success, *Camp Rock*!

Being as popular as they are, would they ever – shock horror – split up to go solo? Luckily, says Joe, that would never happen. "For us, it would never be a solo project, it'd be a side project," he says. "There's no way we can just break up, because, I mean, I live in the same house as them, so it's going to be pretty difficult." Phew!

So for now, just sit back
and enjoy the ride, as these
brothers are going to be
around for a long time!

Crossword – p.40

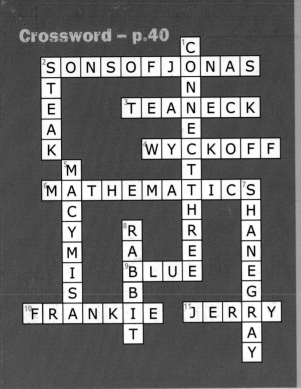

Quiz – p.12

1. a) Kevin, b) Nick, c) Joe, d) Frankie
2. c) His feet
3. a) Casa Grande, Arizona
4. d) Can boss his brothers around
5. b) *It's About Time*
6. d) Mexico
7. a) James Dean
8. c) Peter Pan
9. a) Have a dance party – turning everything up as loud as it will go
10. c) Starbucks
11. d) Blue
12. a) *High School Musical*
13. c) Diabetes
14. b) Falling off the stage
15. a) Frankie
16. a) The iTunes store
17. c) Connect Three
18. d) Mathematics
19. a) Shane Gray
20. c) Paul Kevin Jonas Senior and Denise Jonas

First published in hardback in Great Britain in 2009 by Orion Books an imprint of the Orion Publishing Group Ltd Orion House, 5 Upper St Martin's Lane, London WC2H 9EA An Hachette UK Company

10 9 8 7 6 5 4 3 2 1

A CIP catalogue record for this book is available from the British Library.

ISBN: 978 1 4091 1331 7

Designed by www.carrstudio.co.uk
Printed in Spain by Rotolito Lombardo

The Orion Publishing Group's policy is to use papers that are natural, renewable and recyclable and made from wood grown in sustainable forests. The logging and manufacturing processes are expected to conform to the environmental regulations of the country of origin.

ACKNOWLEDGEMENTS

Posy Edwards would like to thank Helia Phoenix, Amanda Harris, Helen Ewing, James Martindale, Jane Sturrock, Frank Brinkley, and Rich Carr.

PICTURE CREDITS

Getty: 2, 3, 4, 5, 6, 7, 10, 12, 13, 14, 16, 17, 18, 22, 24, 25, 23, 26, 27 (bottom), 28 (top), 30, 29, 44, 45, 46, 47, 48, 49, 50, 51, 52, 53, 54 (top), 55, 56, 57 (right), 58, 59, 60, 61

Rex: 32, 33, 34, 35, 36, 37, 38, 39, 38, 41, 42 (top)

PA Photos: 8, 9, 11, 15, 27 (top), 28 (bottom), 42 (bottom), 54 (bottom), 57 (left & middle)